ARTISTS ARE WEIRD BUT WRITERS ARE CRAZY

DARA GIRARD

CONTENTS

Introduction	v
1. The Beggar Class	1
2. A Mistaken Mystique	9
3. Ready–Fire–Aim!	19
4. Tortoise versus Hare	25
5. The Dark Side	35
6. Forget Everybody	43
7. Cultivate Your Own Garden	51
8. The Whine of Why	57
9. Where You Stand	63
10. Hiring Strangers	69
11. The Originator	77
12. The Rock and the River	83
Intro to Bonus Chapter	89
13. The Canvas and the Keyboard	91
Also Available	103
About the Author	105

Artists are Weird but Writers are Crazy

Copyright © 2022 Sadé Odubiyi

Portions of this book were first published in 2011 and 2012 in a slightly different version on daragirard.com

ISBN 13: 978-1-949764-56-7

Published by ILORI Press Books

Cover Design and Layout Copyright © 2022 ILORI Press Books

Cover design by ILORI Press Books

Cover Image Copyright ©A-R-T-U-R/depositphotos

All rights reserved. No part of this publication may be reproduced, stored in a retrieval system, or transmitted in any form or by any means, electronic, mechanical, recording or otherwise, without the prior written permission of the author.

DISCLAIMER

This book is not intended to provide professional advice and is sold with the understanding that the publisher and the author are not liable for the misconception or misuse of the information provided. The author and ILORI Press Books, LLC shall have neither liability nor responsibility to any person or entity with respect to any loss, damage, or injury caused or alleged to be caused directly or indirectly by the information provided in this book or the use of any products mentioned.

ILORI Press Books, LLC

PO Box #10332

Silver Spring, MD 20914

INTRODUCTION

In 2011, I began a series of blogs under the heading "Artists are Weird BUT Writers are Crazy" after seeing some strange behavior by writers in the publishing industry. But as I saw indie publishing taking hold, I soon abandoned that series, thinking that with new freedom, writers would realize how powerful they are.

Fast forward ten years. I discovered I was wrong. Writers are making even stranger choices than before. (My personal favorite—advice given in a reputable publication—is find all your one-star reviews and change your work accordingly. I didn't know whether to laugh or weep.)

So I looked at this series again with a fresh eye and thought about the conversation that started it all.

August 2010

One day, I was telling my mother (a trained artist)

about a writer who said they don't read because they don't want to be influenced by other writers. They want to be original.

Artist: "Is that common?"

Writer: "Unfortunately, I've met several writers who think that way."

Artist: "That makes no sense. That's like an artist who never looks at the work of other artists or a musician who doesn't listen to music."

Writer: "True, but writers are different."

Artist: "No, writers are crazy..."

I then read *The Wall Street Journal* blog post "Cherish the Book Publishers—You'll Miss Them When They're Gone," which I thought was hilarious until I realized that other writers took it seriously (not serious as in "I'm insulted," but as in "He's right"), that's when I knew what I'd only suspected: Writers are crazy!

But I still wasn't ready to put my thoughts out there until I read a blog post by prolific author Dean Wesley Smith where he said, "Writers, be artists..."

That's when I knew I needed to speak up. He's spot on. Writers can learn a lot from artists.

Some Background

I grew up in a house with an artist. My mother painted a mural on the wall in my bedroom, I had handmade dolls, and I didn't just get notes in my lunch boxes, I got mini masterpieces with cartoons and pictures. I didn't need to buy subject dividers for my school binder; my mother created them for me (my friends were envious and wanted them too).

My mother, a trained medical illustrator, also did abstract painting, created posters, and greeting cards. She made set designs, puppets, dolls, and whatever else her creative mind thought of. Sometimes she sold her work. Sometimes she gave them away, so creative expression was nothing new to me.

From my earliest recollection, I wanted to be a writer (while balancing three other careers, which sounded sensible to a seven-year-old). I created a newsletter at age seven and started sending out my novels to New York editors at twelve (with every intention of getting published by fourteen).

My plan failed, spectacularly.

Looking back, it's no surprise. I loved to read, but I wasn't a great reader (one elementary teacher kept telling me to find easier books to read since I didn't have a "natural aptitude"—I looked up the word and never trusted her again since teaching me anything was not a high priority for her).

Anyway, I had ambition but lacked the skill. I didn't have a natural fluency with language. Few would have thought I'd go on to a life as a writer; I didn't have "natural talent." I missed most of fourth grade recess because I was such a poor speller. In order to motivate us to be better, we had to rewrite every word we got wrong twenty times (well, when you get twenty words wrong, you can image how long that'll take, and no matter how much I tried, certain words kept tripping me up—oh well).

"I don't have talent, I have tenacity."

— HENRY ROLLINS

If nothing else, I hope I can be an example that tenacity beats talent. When you don't know or lack something, with effort, you can learn and improve. That's life's great equalizer that you're not taught in school but works in the real world.

So for years I tried my best not to get buried under the mountain of rejections coming at me. This was the day of snail mail, and I wasn't writing short stories. I was writing one hundred fifty to two hundred–page manuscripts, which kept being boomeranged back to me.

Sometimes the mailbox would be so stuffed with large yellow manila envelopes that the poor mail carrier had to leave the box open or leave them on the front step. Most times I'd race home from school and make sure to get to the mailbox before anyone else did so that I could hide the rejections from my parents. It was hard enough being heartbroken. I knew they'd hurt even more, and I didn't want that—plus they'd worry. For them, the American Dream was not a career as writer. If you're good with words, you become a lawyer—case closed.

But I hung in there for the thirteen years of needed

apprenticeship before I sold my first novel. However, when I finally entered the field as a published author, I was amazed by the fear I encountered. I hadn't experienced it because I'd been on the journey primarily on my own. I hadn't joined critique groups or attended writing workshops and conferences.

I just wrote, submitted, wrote some more, and submitted some more. And when I say wrote, I don't mean just novels or short stories but also poems, plays, essays, articles, ad copy, cards, gags, and so on. I did this for *years* in spite of the puzzled looks of others.

When you're a child, people allow you to dream (isn't that cute?), but by the time I reached my late teens and early twenties, people kept wondering when I'd get over my "little hobby" and grow up and find a real job. (Some still wonder, but that's another story.)

Again, unlike other writers, it took me *years* until I reached my goal of getting a novel published. (I had minor successes with articles and essays being published, but I wanted to be a novelist.) I followed my mother's example. At an early age, she fell in love with art and experimented with different media and styles and created (for years) until she felt comfortable with her craft and expressing herself.

But I soon discovered that writers aren't like that. Writers followed rules whether they made sense or not (no simultaneous submissions—yeah, right). Writers followed critiques (change the hero's career from an accountant to an architect—why?). Writers followed style guides (only use Times New Roman or your work will get rejected—are you serious?). I saw wonderful creative people following arcane rules, constantly seeking validation and confusing art with commerce. I was surprised, but my mother was *horrified*! That's when I saw the stark difference between how an artist thinks and how a writer thinks.

My Goal

Many people think success in publishing is about talent, luck, and hard work. While these may contribute to success, I've found the biggest contributing factor is attitude. Everything else flows from there. I've made a lot of mistakes along the way (A lot. From head shaking to "What was she thinking?"), but I'm still here because of my attitude. I have the "artist mindset." I know that the only time my career stops is when I stop it. Not when someone else tells me it's over. When I create my work, I stand behind it. I'm its biggest advocate. I don't wait for someone else to tell me it's worthy. I say it's worthy first, then look for people who agree. I'm a professional artist who creates with dignity and pride.

And my goal is for other writers to reclaim their dignity. Once you've gone through your growth period (years of writing and rejection from either an editor or the reading public until you write publishable work), you're set. You don't need anyone to still try to "grow" you. One thing my mother taught me was that after enduring six years of criticism from college professors and with her degree in hand, she knew she was a professional artist.

No permission needed.

PLEASE NOTE: This is not to say that artists who haven't gone through a university or art school aren't professionals. Their training may have come from a correspondence course, night classes, or just years of effort. I rarely meet an artist who draws one picture and expects to be deemed a professional. However, I've met many writers who've written one book and stop writing if that one book is rejected. But that's another chapter. The point is an apprenticeship is necessary to hone one's craft—no matter what methods or routes you take.

Throughout this book, I use the term "artist" loosely, more as a mindset rather than as a specific profession. It's not about making "Art" with a capital A; it's about adapting the mindset that will push past the doubts, the insecurities, and the crazy thinking that can get in a writer's way.

And I use the term "indie" to refer to writers who independently publish their work by either self-publishing or creating a company to do so.

Many of the following chapters are edited from the original blog posts. I've put the year it was first posted and then the updated year for clarity and in italics to show what has changed and what hasn't.

Unnecessary Warning

Please note that this series is written in fun. If you don't like hints of sarcasm and hyperbole, don't read this series. If you find the title offensive, don't read this series. However, if you understand that this is a great time to be a writer of fiction and feel like a lone happy person in a tsunami of fear, read on.

THE BEGGAR CLASS

Posted 2011

Crazy Lesson #1

Artists create no matter what. They believe in their work.

Writers look for permission. They wait for someone else to believe in their work before they do.

"Crap is filling the world! Readers won't be able to know what to read because there are so many crappy books out there that they'll stop reading in revolt. We need the agents and editors to save us!"

The above quote is an exaggerated statement I've heard from different people in the industry and was echoed in the *Wall Street Journal* blog by Eric Felten in "Cherish the Book Publishers—You'll Miss Them When They're Gone."

Okay, some agents and editors can believe this rather ridiculous statement (it's their job), but the fact that many writers agree is what frightens me. I started indie publishing before it was cool, when I didn't know how to do e-publishing and stuck with offset printing, using a national distributor, and warehousing my books. During those years (about six years ago), the same statement was said about small/indie publishers: it was believed that we were diluting the pool of quality.

To self-publish was to go around with a scarlet letter S (or V since most people didn't know the difference between self-publishing and vanity publishing—some still don't). You were a loser. Nobody wanted you. I thought this was silly. I self-published because I liked the freedom of creating my own product. I wanted the creative thrill of turning a manuscript into a marketable book. I'd already gone the traditional publishing route and wanted to combine that experience with being independent of the approval process, which more or less looks like this (simplified):

Getting the approval of an **agent**,

then the approval of an **editor**,

then approval of a **sales team/marketing**,

and then **distribution** into bookstores (which is full of more hidden approval processes).

HOW TO REGAIN YOUR SANITY

Take the lead.

Most visual artists don't think they have to go

through a third party to create their product in order to reach their audience. They may choose to do so, but for many they can "set up shop" on the side of a road, in a small coffee shop, or online and show their work. My mother made great money as a teenager selling greeting cards. She didn't go to Hallmark or American Greetings and say, "I'm an aspiring artist with greeting cards. Would you please tell me if they're good enough to go through your line?" No. She created her products and then sold them. Simple.

I followed my mother's example. I wrote a book, had it professionally produced, then sold it through my company. Simple.

The naysayers disagreed. They said: "Oh no. It's not so simple. You're a writer. You must have someone else publish and distribute for you because writers don't know quality and readers will be duped and then your career will be over."

2021 Update: Um...let me clarify one major myth that won't die. Indie publishing didn't start with the creation of the Kindle. Yes, Amazon's Kindle made it much easier for people to enter the field, but before 2009, indie publishing was still an option—sometimes the only option—for people not able to persuade those in New York (Switzerland, London, Vancouver, and so on...) that their stories and voices had a right to be heard.

Beatrix Potter, Charles Dickens, Jane Austen, and Mark Twain all self-published their work, but for a number of reasons, in about the mid-twentieth century (for about thirty years), people were brainwashed into believing that there were only two options to getting published—traditional publishing or vanity publishing.

Vanity publishing was a derogatory term used for anyone who had the audacity to pay to get their work published. So, in this warped thinking, someone who formed their own company (as one person or as a collective) and hired cover designers, copyeditors, interior book designers, and worked with printers to get their work out to the public was lumped with individuals who paid unscrupulous subsidy/vanity press publishers.

Yes, offset printing was costly, using distributors to get into bookstores was a game, but it was doable. Not easy, but not impossible. However, many indie publishers went outside the regular retail channels. Books didn't only sell in bookstores (notice that hasn't changed). Indies of the time would sell direct to readers through the mail, catalogs, at conventions, parties etc. (Think of early hip-hop artists selling tape cassettes out of the trunk of their cars and you get a sense of an entrepreneurial spirit that has always run counter to the mainstream—you won't get on a "list," but you have an audience and money is money—kaching!)

Myths are powerful things. In the US, it's believed that country music rose up from "three chords and the truth" (bwhaa!) and that hip-hop came from streetwise hustlers. (Do you know how many music pioneers/influencers went to college?) I enjoy both types of music and later realized the stories built around them are part of their mystique, but they're still just mythical stories.

A number of people still don't see indie publishing

as a legitimate choice. However, legitimate is a subjective term.

The worldview that those who paid to get published were "vanity publishing" was a very successful way to shame creators into staying in line, to trust authority, and to adhere to certain mandates. Few other fields have successfully convinced creators that they were useless if they didn't go through "sanctioned" channels. Writers were shamed into conformity by the outside world and sadly by each other.

If I sew a dress and wear it, it's no less legit than if I bought it from a retail store. Visual artists who host their own gallery showing and get paid are no less "legit" than those who sell in selected, elite galleries—except in the eyes of those who wish to keep the status quo.

Just like some prolific women writers of pulp fiction have been lost to history because their work wasn't valued, the collective narrative of independent publishing has also been skewed due to "conventional wisdom." (An aside: I recently had someone argue that no female horror writers existed in the past except for Mary Shelley. I told them about the book Monster, She Wrote: The Women Who Pioneered Horror and Speculative Fiction *by Lisa Kroger and Melanie R Anderson and said get back to me. They haven't.)*

I grew up surrounded by and reading many independently published books—some were eventually sold to a big publisher; others you never have heard of, but they made my life rich, inspired me, made me feel less alone, and exposed me to a vast array of people and stories. Fortunately, now the barriers of production and distribution have fallen, it's easier than ever to reach an audience and educate and entertain them; don't let someone else tell you you can't or shouldn't. Remember, if you decide to independently publish your book, you're part of a long, unheralded history. Opportunities have always existed outside the mainstream.

I became a hybrid writer before there was even a word for it, just like Mark Twain did when he got fed up working with publishers. Let the world catch up to you, not the other way around.

Understand that readers are smart.

They will buy what they want. This filter argument is so old it's rotting, but unfortunately, it's brought up every few years as if it's fresh (sort of like the next new diet "secret"). Elitists are always afraid of people having choices, and I've discovered that there are many of them in publishing. To me, life is like a buffet. There are a lot of choices. Choose what you like best. I'm not a big eater, so when I go to a buffet, I don't eat everything I see. I'm selective. I don't just select something because it's there. I may be in the mood to try something new or just go with what I like or go with a friend's suggestion. I certainly don't need someone to select what I should eat based on *their* preferences or limit my choices because they think I'm too feeble minded to choose on my own.

2021 Update: We don't need gatekeepers; we need

curators. Slowly, that field is growing. But to think you need editors and agents to strangle a manuscript before it reaches maturation is just silly.

Understand your purpose.

Writers, your job is to create, not to compare yourself to another writer or worry about what's being put on the market. My mother survived in an industry where an elephant's artwork can sell for five figures. Recently, a four-year-old's painting sold for six! There's even an artist who takes cow dung, puts it on a canvas, and sells it. My mother just shrugs because it doesn't matter. All that matters is what she creates because that's all she can control.

As a writer, your career is based on what you create and the pleasure and information you give. Create, learn, submit, and/or publish. Stop begging for attention, permission, acceptance. Choose your own path. It's one golden link to sanity.

2021 Update: Publishing was strange ten years ago. It's dangerous now. With so many draconian contracts, distribution issues, mergers (I'm looking at you Penguin Random House and Simon & Schuster), and lack of forward thinking in terms of the use of intellectual property, I think it behooves a new writer to really think about whether sending their work to a traditional publisher is a savvy long-term strategy. Do your homework, know what the landscape looks like now, not what it used to look like.

A MISTAKEN MYSTIQUE

Posted 2011

I recently spoke to an agent interested in a general fiction book I'd written who wanted me to spend five years revising it. Not five weeks or five months, but five YEARS. I thought she was insane. She thought I wasn't committed to excellence and told me of another client of hers who spent that amount of time on one book and became an Oprah Magazine Book Pick.

I like Oprah, but there's no way I'm going to spend my creative energy trying to rewrite something just to please the sensibilities of someone else. The problem with the agent's suggestion was that she was completely clueless as to how stories are created. Many writers fall into this trap. I've met numerous writers who will spend months polishing three chapters to enter into a contest or others who've spent ten to twenty years on one "masterpiece" because writing is supposed to be painful;

> ***"Don't ever write a novel unless it hurts like a hot turd coming out."***
>
> — CHARLES BUKOWSKI

a struggle;

> ***"Writing is easy. All you do is sit down at a typewriter and open a vein."***
>
> — RED SMITH

or difficult.

> ***"I'd never encourage anyone to be a writer. It's too hard."***
>
> — EUDORA WELTY

(Cue in ominous music and the voice of Vincent Price from Michael Jackson's song "Thriller".)

Discouragement, pain, heartbreak, obscurity, that's the writer's lot so be FOREWARNED. Most of this is baloney because the one thing many people forget is that great writers know how to lie. (They're storytellers, remember?) And it serves a purpose because writers need to feel important, which leads me to:

. . .

Crazy Lesson #2

Artists believe they can create at their own pace.
Writers believe they have to create slowly.

There are three reasons for this insanity: the education system, the industry, and writers themselves.

The Education System

Visual artists have an advantage. I've envied that advantage all my life. If someone asked to see my mother's work, all she had to do was go to her portfolio or point to something on the wall, and within *seconds*, her work could be seen.

Not so with me. First, few people ever ask to see my work, and I know why. There's a bigger investment of time and attention. Even if it is a five-page short story, someone has to set energy aside to invest in my work. This is why art professors and writing professors view creativity in different ways—time isn't an issue for art teachers the way it is for writing teachers. Here's when "time" became a factor in the writer's creative process.

An art professor can go through fifty art students' work and give an opinion. A writing professor doesn't have that luxury. So to help save time and their eyesight, they decided to equate effort (i.e. time spent) with quality. If you were the type of student bursting with ideas and wanted to hand in essays and stories every week, they'd likely say, "Are you sure you're finished?" "Did you *really* do your best?" "You don't want to be like those hack writers who type out garbage. Go back and take your time." Somehow the saying "True writing is rewriting" has become the guideline by which most writers are measured.

And unfortunately these statements feed the Doubt Demon in your head and you start to question your process. I know. I've been there. But the basic fact is these instructors don't want to have too many papers to grade. Granted, there are great teachers (thanks, Mr. D!) who encourage productivity, but most don't (and some are struggling, heartbroken writers themselves, so they think this is the truth that needs to be taught). So writing slow is an *advantage* to the education system, but not to the writer who only learns by writing—a lot.

The Industry

In the past, publishers believed that books from the same author competed against each other, so they encouraged writers to produce a limited number—one or two (at most)—a year. (I'm speaking in generalities. I know that in category fiction, this isn't true.) Some agents also believed this, but for an entirely different reason: slow writers equal less work. I have nothing against agents as a whole (individually, that's another story), but I do have a problem with CCK Agents, which I like to dub as Creativity/Career-Killing Agents. I once sent four books (with synopses and proposals) to an agent who sat on them for six months before telling me that she was only going to focus on selling them one at a time. Here's a little secret: the more books you sell, the more money you make.

So, not only was I having my creativity squelched, my income was dropping, too. Needless to say, I (amicably) parted ways, went back to writing and submitting (working with an IP lawyer to look over my contracts), and saw my creativity and income level rise again. (The first time this happened, I didn't learn my lesson. I had to have two more times of income dropping and creativity flat line before I made the connection.) Fortunately, in the new industry (e-publishing, print on demand, audio), the reality of the power of creativity and productivity is clearly evident. Numerous books from one author don't compete with each other and crumble a writer's career; they build and strengthen it.

The slow writer has to depend on luck (and we all know how promiscuous that lady is). The prolific author doesn't have to worry about luck because as they improve their craft they build an audience by planting many seeds. The more work they have available, the more opportunities they give readers to find them. The one-book method means you must be discovered and loved immediately.

Now, I'm not saying you *have* to write fast. (Do whatever makes you happy.) I'm just saying that if you do, don't feel bad or try to change for anyone.

. . .

Writers

Yes, we're to blame, too. We've created our own madness. Why?

Because many of us are desperate for validation because we've lost our mystique. When my mother says "I'm an artist" or "I'm a trained medical illustrator," people are impressed.

On the other hand, when I say that I'm a writer, people say things like:

"My five-year-old writes stories, too."

"I have an idea I could give you to write and we could split the profits."

"No, really. What do you do for a living?"

No one is impressed because ANYONE can write. To gain back some semblance of respect, many authors have to make writing appear as something difficult and IMPORTANT. They have to make it sound like a tedious job. To their detriment, many aspiring authors will feel guilty and work hard until they hate writing and think, "Ah, yes! This is what being a writer is all about."

That's insane. Let me tell you what's hard. I've had many interesting experiences in my life, and I'll share a few. Telling someone that his daughter is going to die is hard; wiping up vomit from three sick kids in a hot summer camp latrine is hard; listening to a woman screaming on the other end of a 911 call as her husband beats her is hard. I've done all three, and believe me, I'd rather be writing.

HOW TO REGAIN YOUR SANITY

Thank goodness there's hope. Here are four options:

Keep the curtain closed.

Don't let anyone tell you what your process *should* be. Are you a plotter or panster? Do you write in the morning or at night? Do you outline or use a spreadsheet? It doesn't matter. Do whatever you need to so you can get the work done. If you write fast, that's fine. If you write slow, that's fine, too. Either way, don't feel superior or inferior, because your method is not important. Your ideal is whatever works for you and helps you to speed past the Doubt Demon, gives a rude gesture to the Critic, and gets you to keep your creativity fresh and fun. All that matters is the finished product.

Don't allow trespassers.

Only work with people who will keep their filthy paws off your creative process. It's none of their business how you work. That means family, friends, critique partners, editors, agents, publicists, and other writers. I trust my first reader and copyeditor because they know their place. They make comments on the manuscript, but that's it. If anyone tells you how you should work, what your process should be, edits out your voice, or puts you down in anyway, move on.

Realize it's not important.

I'm sorry, but the process of creation doesn't matter as much as people want it to. All professional writers know this. Whether you feel brilliant or stupid, you can come up with great scenes. I've written novels when I was under the weather, during family crises, deaths, stress, and times of great joy. Thankfully, my readers won't be able to tell which book was written when. The final product doesn't depend on your moods, your process, or your environment.

It's true in all arts.

My mother is not a desk artist. She doesn't like sitting too long at the drafting table or standing at her easel. A friend of hers could spend two hours drawing a single line, but their work is comparable. You wouldn't be able to tell which took two months and which took two weeks. (I've never seen them comparing notes.) Each of them does their work in their own way, and that's it.

Creativity is a mystical thing. Let your subconscious take over and let the magic happen.

Lie.

This is the best way to keep sane. Lie with a smile.

Give people the stories they want to hear. Tell them the struggle you experienced trying to come up with a plot, how you cried when you killed off the turtle, how it took you two years to get through a scene. I don't care what you say, as long as you're happy and entertaining people. Lie, like the rest of us. If you're asked to do a rewrite, don't send it in the next day. Let it sit for several weeks, then hand it in. Life will be easier that way.

Lie, lie, lie! Lie to everyone, except to yourself. Call your writing "work" to outsiders, but consider it "play," "practice," "fun" to yourself.

You know the truth; you know your process and what works. Keep the magic alive—you won't regret it.

READY-FIRE-AIM!

Posted 2011

Are you sitting on the fence about an idea you want to pursue? Then this post is for you.

I recently had a conversation with a fellow writer that went something like this:

"Hey, Dara, I've got a great idea for a new book." (proceeds to tell me the idea)

"Wonderful," I say, knowing that ideas, like dust, are everywhere. "Get started."

"I can't. There's a problem."

"What? Is your system down? Then use a pen and paper or talk into a recorder or..."

"No, it's not that. It's so different from what I usually write."

"So?" I say. "Write it anyway."

"I'm under contract to write my usual work."

"Write it on the side."

"I'm not sure my agent will like it. She says that I should focus on writing (current trend)."

I sigh. "Your agent doesn't have to like it. Write it first, and then worry about it later."

"But what if I write it and then can't sell it?"

By now I'm trying not to grit my teeth. "Why are you worrying about something that hasn't even happened yet?"

"But it could happen…"

At this point, I lose my patience, so I'll save you from my less-than-polite reply. The point is that this conversation, and conversations like them, both irritate and scare me. Why?

Crazy Lesson #3

Artists create what they want and then market it.
Writers think of a market first and then create.

Talk about a creativity killer.
You can't discover new things this way. You can't develop new genres or storytelling styles.

You don't need permission to create.
You don't need permission to grow.
You don't need permission to experiment.

Seeking permission gives you someone to blame.

I remember sending a proposal to an editor who passed on the premise. I'm still going to write the book because I WANT TO. I, the creative artist, like the idea and believe others will, too. (I never think of whether or not a large audience will agree with me; that's not my problem or focus.)

2021 Update: I wrote the book and published it myself. I know, I know this "being an artist" advice makes no business sense to many indie writers. I once heard a writer say that being creative nearly destroyed their career because they wrote something they loved and nobody read it. Okay, it had been on the market only three months and was in a completely different genre than what they were known for, but they came to the conclusion that taking risks is for naïve people.

I won't try to convince anyone. Many writers are even more market driven despite the freedom indie publishing provides. They are presently very successful being market-driven, and I say if you can successfully create for decades based on outside whims, more power to you. For those who want to continue to grow, to start a trend instead of follow one, to discover new things, please understand that you can run your business and, with the right strategy, try many different things and keep your creative mind happy, free, and well-fed.

In publishing, editors and agents act as managers. They like to keep the status quo. They like to use what has sold in the past to help predict what *they* believe will sell in the future. When it comes to a new release, they care about making the biggest splash possible. (There's no long-term planning in publishing.) So if your book is "too unique" or your audience "too small," they're not interested. Or they'll kindly encourage you to water your text down to make it more mainstream. That's their job, not yours. When I was traditionally published, my editor did a good job of reining me in to suit the tastes of their particular audience. No problem! I know that's her job. But her suggestions did not stop me from writing with a wild abandon each time I started a new book either for them or for myself because I was careful never to let "outside" voices intrude into my creative process.

If you, as a writer, put their "marketing limitations" in your mind, good luck staying true to yourself and writing stories that will resonate with your particular audience or even an audience you'd never considered.

2021 Update: Nothing much has changed from the statement above except that traditional publishing is employing even more short-term thinking than in the past while also gobbling up rights that they don't know what to do with. Meanwhile, many indies have fallen for market-driven thinking, too. They like to look at the current landscape and write as if it's fixed and will never change...until a renegade writer changes it and then everyone follows suit...

HOW TO REGAIN YOUR SANITY

Don't be afraid to be wrong.

If you want to write something, write it. Test. Experiment. Nothing is ever wasted. It's practice, learning, growth. You won't know what will work until you try it.

Know that true artists are game changers.

They don't follow, they lead. They create *first*, then worry about who their art will serve. If you want to be compliant (rewrite until your voice is gone, write what someone else tells you), that's fine (sad, but fine). You'll never stand out and your unique voice will be unnecessarily smothered. And the joy I like to talk about will quickly disappear.

Understand that storytellers rule.

Storytellers are at their most powerful when they're courageous enough to tell the stories in their hearts. They may not make a big splash in the beginning, but they will eventually get noticed by those they're meant to serve. *Star Trek* didn't gain its rabid following until it was in re-runs. The classic movie *It's a Wonderful Life* wasn't a holiday staple until decades after its release. *The Great Gatsby*, *Their Eyes Were Watching God*, and other notable titles were put out of print while their authors were alive but were later "rediscovered." If they hadn't created these works, we wouldn't be talking about them.

Take calculated risks.

You won't destroy your career. Careers are more resilient than you think. Many long-term professionals have had to reinvent or pivot many times. Adaptability is the secret sauce, not stagnation. Also, by stretching yourself, you'll become better at your craft.

You'll learn more about yourself and about your world.

Write, create, submit, and repeat: Fire as many new, wonderful stories that you can. You may fail, you may succeed. That's the point. You're a working writer —that's what we do.

TORTOISE VERSUS HARE

Posted 2011

In a previous post, I described how many writers have been brainwashed into thinking that the pace in which they produce their work matters. Today I'll talk about a different type of pace: sales! Many writers have been brainwashed into thinking that fast sales mean a book is good, while slow sales mean a book is bad.

Crazy Lesson #4

Artists create and sell at their own pace.
Writers believe they have to write slow but sell fast.

Velocity is a publishing buzzword and a critical component in the traditional publishing model, which has to deal with limited shelf space in brick-and-mortar stores. Velocity sales equal books that sell fast within the first several weeks. Selling fast means a book has a chance to hit a bestseller's list (which focuses on the short-term life of a book, not the long term) or helps convince a bookstore to keep a particular title stocked. In traditional publishing, fast sales have been translated to mean that a book is alive and worthy of attention and support; slows sales mean that a book will be pulled from the shelves and remaindered or destroyed and, worst yet, the author is dropped if they produce too many slow-selling books.

In traditional publishing, books are looked at as perishable products, like milk and yogurt, with sell-by dates. This thinking forced authors to believe that their books could spoil if they didn't sell at a certain pace.

Gone are the days when an author could grow their audience and skill. Gone are stories of authors like Jack Higgins who wrote twenty-some books before hitting it big with *The Eagle Has Landed* or Nora Roberts who wrote nearly sixty romance novels over ten years before hitting the *New York Times* list.

No, in traditional publishing, books are considered produce (explained brilliantly by author Dean Wesley Smith in his blog post Books Are No Longer Produce). This model suits publishers who deal in volume, but it's not good for authors. This limiting viewpoint is to the detriment of new voices. Without a backlist, authors can't build word of mouth or gain new skills. Readers are forced to go to used bookstores to find authors they've liked who've strangely disappeared or who write quirky books that don't fit the mainstream.

In his (out-of-print) book *How to Write Bestselling*

Fiction, Dean Koontz aptly said, "Unimaginative editors and publishers think that every bestselling author must spring up in full bloom, smashing onto the bestseller list his first time out."

And if an author doesn't hit it big after several—say two—books? "Many editors say, 'He just doesn't have what it takes.'"

Suddenly, that author has a big L on their chest (for loser, limited talent, you choose), and editors and agents label them that for the rest of their career, not understanding that writers can grow and improve, if given the chance. To be fair, most people in entertainment like quick labels. (Thinking takes too much effort.) Think of the brilliant minds who labeled Katherine Hepburn "box-office poison," called Jon Cryer of *Two and Half Men* fame "a series killer," or the producer who saw an episode of *Star Trek* and referred to it as "tits in space" (but that's another topic).

What the traditional publishing industry has never understood is this:**books don't die.**

Enter the beauty of indie publishing where authors can create without the pressure of trying to sell lots of books within six weeks.

Unfortunately, most writers don't see this, and many indie publishers are putting this pressure on themselves. I see authors checking their rankings nearly every hour, spending lots of time and sometimes enormous amounts of money promoting one book instead of writing others. Some indie publishers price their products as cheaply as possible so that they can reach a large number of readers. (Done strategically, this is a great business model or if you're a discount publisher more power to you. But if you're pricing your work cheaply just because you're desperate, I don't see "long-term writing career" in your future.)

I know it's hard being a turtle in a world filled with hares. Most people know the statement "slow and steady wins the race," but few believe it. I want you to take a deep breath and know that this statement is true. As people race past you, don't despair. Your time will come, and you'll hit the finish line.

Remember, books don't die. I'm not saying that selling fast is bad. However, confusing fast sales with quality is dangerous thinking. Why? Because...

Speed Thinking Kills Hopes. Especially with new authors who want instant gratification. They put something up and expect it to sell 25,000 copies in three weeks and then get depressed when it doesn't.

Speed Thinking Kills Creativity. People who focus on sales start to worry about trends. Trying to cash in on someone else's success is just sad. Readers don't need imitators; they need storytellers.

Speed Thinking Kills Productivity. Too much time and effort spent marketing one project takes away from creating others.

Speed Thinking Kills Camaraderie. When writers start worrying about lists, they enter a competitive mode because there are limited slots on a list.

Again, there are those authors who are meant to sell fast. They'll always sell fast, and I applaud them. They are doing their job and making people happy. This post, however, is for those authors who may not sell fast until the fifth book or tenth book or sixtieth. Keep writing and stop worrying about what you cannot control. I've seen authors spend thousands of dollars marketing their work and still not sell well. That doesn't necessarily mean the book is bad; it may not have been found by the right audience yet.

Visual artists don't throw a canvas away just because it didn't sell fast. They wait for the right buyer while they work on other projects. My mother has a painting from forty years ago. It didn't sell then (too radical for its time), but I bet she could find a buyer now. In the seventies, she started creating greeting cards depicting portraits of children. Many decades later, if she wanted to, she can still sell them. Quality lasts.

HOW TO REGAIN YOUR SANITY

Remember everything has a season.

Writing a book and then worrying about how fast it sells is like planting a seed, then standing over it with a stopwatch shouting, "Grow, dammit, grow!" If it doesn't grow at the speed you want it to, you may panic and overwater it or recklessly pull it up and throw it out because you think it's useless, when it just needed more time to take root.

As a writer, each book, story, essay is like a planted seed. Leave it and plant others. You never know which one will bloom first. You may never have a prize-winning pumpkin, but if you plant enough seeds, one day you'll have an amazing harvest.

Books are always new.

I recently read a book that was published in 1978 and loved it. It was new to me. Each book will be new to a reader who's never experienced it before. Think of all the children who've never read *Madeline* or *Anne of Green Gables* or *Harry Potter*. It doesn't matter when the book was printed.

While *A Christmas Carol* by Charles Dickens remained in print, all of Jane Austen's work had been out of print for years until "rediscovered." Imagine *Pride and Prejudice* or *Emma* never getting a chance to reach a new audience.

There are a host of books that regained new life when someone read them and championed them. The stories didn't change; their readers did. Remember, books—or rather stories—don't die. Stories remain fresh to new eyes. So don't worry when a book sells slowly. Be too busy working on your next project.

Update 2021: Another example of this is the children's book Goodnight Moon. *Initially considered "overly sentimental," it was not a breakout success when it was first released in 1947. Far from it. It had pitiful sales. However, many years later, when the kids who'd grown up with the story had kids of their own, they bought the book in droves, and the rest is history.*

Readers take their time.

I love to read, but there are so many books that I will not get to this year or next. There will be gems published this year that I won't get to until perhaps five to ten years from now. I hope they'll still be available for sale because I like to discover and read new authors at my *own* pace, not a pace dictated by publishers.

Update 2021: Streaming makes this even more evident. I'll watch, read, and listen to what I want when I want to. However, there are some indies unpublishing work they deem failures because of slow or low sales! Ahh...as a reader, I can't begin to tell you how annoying that trend is.

I'd just started a series that I liked, then the author removed all the books from every retailer. Fortunately, my library still had digital versions available to read, but I would have paid her if she'd kept her work available in the retail market. One marketing expert said that a book needs to have fifty reviews within six months to survive the online retail market machine. Sorry, but I actually have ancient books (translation: ten years old) that don't have a lot of reviews but are still selling and finding new readers. I think having a portfolio of work really does matter, but perhaps I'm naïve, and I'm far from an expert.

A fast rise can mean a fast fall.

This doesn't always happen, but sometimes it does. Many authors who shoot to the top with their debut novel have this awful event called Second Book Syndrome. The author becomes paralyzed by the success of their first book and feels pressured to match it with their next book. I'm always saddened when I hear about authors who suffer this fate. I think it happens because they're no longer writing from a pure state of joy, but instead they're thinking about things outside of their control such as, "Will this book be as good as the last?" "What will readers think?" and so on. That kind of thinking is deadly to creativity.

A slow build allows an author to try different skills, hone their strengths, and cover their weaknesses. They can grow into their role as a working writer, instead of being branded the author of one particular type of book and not given the chance to branch out.

Times are changing.

As a fiction writer, you're in a world full of choices. You can write for big publishers (with caution), small publishers (also caution), the digital publishers (you get the drill), micropublishers, and/or self-publish. You can write under different names. You can have one half of your career worry about fast sales (i.e. traditional where you have to sell within six months or less) while your other half slowly builds an audience (indie publishing where your title may not even start hitting traction until after six months to a year).

Update 2021: I foolishly thought indies would approach publishing in a whole new way, but they seem to have become more fearful than before. One thing I didn't expect was a lack of patience. Selling fast still seems to be the name of the game, especially in indie publishing. They're spending thousands on promotion. Some work, some don't, but few indies will make that distinction. Promotion is everything—not story, not consistency, nothing. Just promotion. I'll deal with that in a later chapter, but I find it sad that the value of a piece of work is being based on velocity of sales.

Pen names are not what they used to be. Brand your work right and you can write under one name. Again, do your homework because this takes strategy. Every new genre will be a different career to manage. You won't necessarily have a crossover audience, so plan wisely. Decide on the kind of writer you wish to be and the type of career you wish to have. The world of choices continues to expand.

Inventory trumps speed.

One of the most beautiful compliments a reader can say to a writer is, "What's next?" If an author only has one or two books for sale, readers will go elsewhere. Now if you don't want to have a long writing career, then go ahead and depend on luck and focus on one book hitting it big.

But if you want to be a working writer, remember that your job is to create as much inventory as possible so that you can confidently answer the question "What's next?" over and over again. Like a dandelion, spread your seeds in many places. People will stumble upon you.

One of your books may take off like a rocket, but you'll be too busy to care.

THE DARK SIDE

Posted 2012

"Every time you think you've been screwed by publishers in every possible way, you meet one who has read the Kama Sutra."

— CATHY CRIMSONS

Writers have opinions—especially about other writers. Michael Stackpole refers to them as "house slaves," in his blog post "Swimming Lessons for House Slaves: No One Will Swim for You."

Sarah Hoyt compares them to abused wives, as in her blog post "He Beats Me But He's My Publisher," while others just thinks they're stupid (but they're doing their best to help).

You already know what I think. I think writers are

crazy. And some, in this group, seem to be confusing themselves with ladies of the night.

> ***"Writing is like prostitution. First you do it for the love of it, then you do it for a few friends, and finally you do it for the money."***
>
> — MOLIERE

And obviously the publishing world agrees. Publishers seem to be in a race to create The Best Little Whore House—I mean The Best Assisted Self-publishing House—in the city.

Companies like Penguin's new "assisted self-publishing" Book Country is nothing new. Like Harlequin Horizons—I mean Dellarte Press (now closed)—you get to choose (i.e. pay for) different self-publishing packages, and because they're being so good to you, they'll also take a percentage of your royalty. Now doesn't that sound fair? Sure...like bending over to get screwed, then paying for that brief moment (pleasure?) for the rest of your life sounds fair.

Update 2021: There are so many different assisted self-publishing companies you can find them on your own with one simple search. This trend is alive and well, and I won't even include agents who are now also publishers because there's so much wrong with that arrangement. But maybe I'm missing something.

Writer: "But Dara, they're publishers, and they could help me get my work out."

A statement like this leads me to my next lesson for writers.

Crazy Lesson #5

Artists place value on their work.
Writers place value on their publishers.

Okay, think of an artist getting her work professionally framed. Proper framing is important because showing one's art is about presentation. A good frame makes a piece of artwork more marketable. It's essential and takes a special skill.

So let's look a little closer. Say an artist gets their work framed, and then the framer says, "Now pay me $500 for the frame and each licensing right you sell."

Yes, that's right. Now what the "framer" is saying to the artist is, "When I frame your work, I now own it (the copyright). If you create a lithograph, use the image on a bookmark, on a poster, a wall hanging, floor tiles, or plates, then I expect to see a cheque in the mail for every sale made because I *framed* that picture and helped make it marketable. You couldn't do it without me."

The artist would walk away.

The writer, however, in a similar situation (i.e.

taking a raw manuscript and putting it into a book format), says:

"Sign me up."

"Sign me up to pay for a service I can do myself for free."

"Charge me exorbitant fees because I'm too lazy—I mean tired/scared/uncertain—to find out what different services really cost."

"Take my rights away with a smile and a promise that you'll hold my hand through the entire process because I know that my work means more to you than pleasing the shareholders."

"I need you because I'm just a lowly writer and you're a big powerful publisher who will look out for me and protect me from scam artists."

When I recently told a friend of mine about "assisted self-publishing" and some of the shady promises publishers are promoting, he replied, "Oh yeah. They're like pimps, right?" I paused, a little stunned by the comparison (I have...ahem interesting friends), then had to think for a minute. He had a point.

Prostitutes (rent boys, fill in the blank) make the same argument as some writers do for why they need pimps. They do all the work and pay the pimp for "protection."

"At least I have a pimp. You don't know how scary it is without one. He takes good care of me."

"It's hard being out there on your own. I'm not smart enough."

"I can make more money with a pimp than without one."

And of course the pimps love this loyalty because it's not that hard to get. Once you get one prostitute, you keep her pay low (and sometimes the drug addiction high) so that you keep her under control. And you remind her how she'll never make it without you.

Pimps, excuse me, some publishers do the same. They keep the writer's pay low (tying up as many rights that they can) and keep the fear level high so that they keep writers under control.

Update 2021: In indie publishing the new pimp is called promotion. And this pimp is making hundreds of thousands out of the gross revenue for a number of indies. For some reason, many indies have the same refrain as traditionally published writers. "I can't live without it." "I won't be safe without it."

Unfortunately, many indies do not understand what promotion really is. Promotion is just one of the four Ps of Marketing. The other three include price, product, and place.

Also there are five types of promotion, but indies tend to focus on one—advertising. Many industry gurus have brainwashed writers into believing their work will live or die by this one metric. However, making sure you have good sales copy, covers that match the genre (understanding what genre is) placement, pricing, and the other types of promotion will get indies off this expensive merry-go-round. Yes, you do need promotion, just not the way you think.

HOW TO REGAIN YOUR SANITY

Do your homework.

First, with the internet available 24/7, there's no excuse not to do your research. I mean real research, not just looking at the first three links that come up with an online search. Let's be honest, the internet is not a vast wasteland with hidden gems of knowledge. You have to do some digging. However, it's worth the effort. You will find there are some GREAT services out there if you want to independently publish. Learn about them.

Second, please understand that you're not just in the book industry. You're in the intellectual rights industry. Get a copy of *The Copyright Handbook*. Your story is more than just words—it's an enterprise (think sub-rights like audio, large print, dramatic, foreign). Understand that one story can mushroom into an industry. Don't believe me? Then please tell me what *Harry Potter*, *Diary of a Wimpy Kid*, or *Twilight* are all about.

Third, know that nobody really cares. It's not because they're mean, but publishing is all about business. If someone can make money off of your ignorance, they will. If I were heartless, I could make a lucrative living fleecing writers of their good hard cash. Think I'm kidding? One assisted self-publisher in the US charges $204.00 for copyright registration, another closer to $400. If you do it yourself, you only pay a fraction of that.

Check out https://www.copyright.gov/registration/

Stop seeking validation.

Readers don't care about publishers. They care about good stories. I recently read a great book I enjoyed, and I remember the author's name but not who published it. Why? Because I don't care. As a reader, do you only read books by one publisher? Are you loyal to publishers or authors? You don't need permission to be a published author. You don't need someone to anoint you. Yes, it's good for the ego for about a day but really not necessary. Your job is to write. Make your work available for readers, whether traditionally and/or not, and then write your next work. That's it. Repeat, repeat, repeat.

Respect yourself.

If you don't respect yourself, why should anyone else? If you don't realize you're holding a golden nugget and sell it to someone for the price of brass, that's your fault, not theirs. Your stories matter. Your ability to make a living from your work matters. Recognizing your weakness and partnering with people who have your best interest in mind matters. Knowing who they are versus the charlatans matters.

Don't let insecurities and fears force you to fall for the fairy tale that someone with a thousand potential clients will be your new best friend. That they'll look out for you. If you don't respect yourself and become savvy in business, no one else will.

FORGET EVERYBODY

Posted 2012

Two words I despise, especially in publishing, are "everybody" and "nobody."

Everybody is on Facebook.
Everybody has a smartphone.
Everybody drives a car.
Nobody knows about eating a banana wrapped in rice.
Nobody knows what a dumpling is.
Nobody listens to (watches, reads, enjoys) *that* anymore.

Crazy Lesson #6
Artists believe in breaking rules.
Writers believe in keeping rules.

2021 Update: Because some writers like to nitpick, I'll be as clear as possible on this topic. The following post is based on the understanding that you know the difference between being a freelancer and being an entrepreneur. If you've been hired to fulfill a contract of any kind, there are likely certain rules/guidelines you have to follow.

Readers have expectations, and a savvy writer understands this. They know the difference between a love story and a romance. (Some people still think "The Tragedy of Romeo and Juliet" is a romance, completely missing the word "tragedy." There are tragic love stories but no tragic romances. Trust me, romance readers expect happy endings; those who like love stories enjoy when death separates the lovers.) Some indies put fantasy elements on the covers of science fiction novels. Others put happy smiling people on thrillers and wonder why sales are sluggish. Um...

Trying to flaunt the expectations of an established genre isn't being an "artist." It's being disrespectful and will likely frustrate you (you'll think the readers are stupid) and anger readers (they'll never buy you again). But sometimes writers who misunderstand what being an artist means will plunge ahead in spite of this. (I mean, sure, if you can fill a children's book with swear words or a cozy mystery with sexually explicit content and get away with it, hats off to you.)

Freelance artists follow the instructions of those who hire them. It's called being professional. However, when it comes to their own work...

Most artists don't paint by numbers or worry about staying in the lines. They don't mind focusing on a niche audience. If a larger group doesn't understand what they're doing, that's not their problem. They don't explain themselves; they create to their own standards.

Writers, on the other hand, are constantly looking for validation from the largest audience possible, and they will twist their creative muse into a pretzel (kill it if necessary) to get to that supposed elevated place. Now don't get me wrong, I'm not saying that authors who reach a large audience have "sold out." Far from it. There are master storytellers who can enchant millions. Good for them. Just like there are artists who do the same. That's great. However, I think of the quote by Henry Van Dyke:

"Use what talents you possess; the woods would be very silent if no birds sang there except those that sang best."

As a writer, you may not reach millions, or hundreds of thousands, but that doesn't mean your art has no value. And who knows, as your craft and your productivity grows, your audience may grow, too. But even if it doesn't, the joy you bring to the few is just as important as to the many. Artists understand this. Many writers don't.

Personally, I really hate writing for Everybody—this bastard always gets in the way of telling a good story. I decided to indie publish before the present boom because I wanted to write for Somebody. Somebody may not be as well known as Everybody, but she's always been interesting to me.

Sometimes she shops at a discount or thrift store. Sometimes she speaks a different language or dialect. I certainly prefer her to Nobody. To me, Nobody is boring, stupid, and fearful.

It's not all the writer's fault. They believe in catering to Everybody and try to avoid Nobody. We've been brainwashed into believing that creating blockbusters is all that matters and serving the masses is paramount.

We have been told that the masses (i.e. Everybody) like things simple, watered down, and easily digestible. Because publishing is an industry about the bottom line, all that matters is creating products (not art) that reaches as many people as fast as possible.

Which is fine if you're a factory worker creating interchangeable widgets, not an artist. Especially not if you're a content creator building a portfolio. It's dangerous for a writer to sweep a group of individuals with one brush and put them into stereotypical cages. It kills their individuality. Not all gays are liberals. Not everyone in the South is one step away from being a redneck or likes country music. Not all Asians are brilliant mathematicians. (A friend of mine failed trigonometry with spectacular results.) Not every Black person has great rhythm. (Trust me!)

While growing up, I didn't realize how useful it was going to be to be an "outsider" (i.e. the child of immigrants: in school, instead of "The Star-Spangled

Banner," I knew the lyrics to "God Save the Queen") until I stepped out as a storyteller. New York, London, Vancouver, and Los Angeles kept telling me that my stories weren't real. Nobody talks like that. Nobody acts like that. Everybody does this (fill in the blank). But I knew they were wrong because Nobody and Everybody kept ignoring Somebody—me!

HOW TO REGAIN YOUR SANITY

"Listen carefully to first criticisms of your work. Note just what it is about your work that critics don't like—then cultivate it. That's the part of your work that's individual and worth keeping."

— JEAN COCTEAU

Protect your stories.

Forget about trying to reach Everybody and avoiding Nobody. Unless you're an insecure teenager (*Everybody's* going to be at the dance! *Nobody* would wear something like that!), that kind of thinking is nonsense and juvenile. As humans, we're a varied and unique group. Remember that lousy clothing label "one size fits all"? Thankfully, most manufactures got a clue and replaced it with "one size fits *most*."

Get your freak on.

Your audience is waiting for your stories. They can't find you until you reveal yourself. It doesn't help them if you sound like Everybody else.

Beware "good intentions."

Someone (who thinks they're doing you a favor) is going to suggest you try to follow the latest trend. They will suggest you dumb down a plot line so you don't alienate readers or they will suggest you rewrite yourself until your voice is "more marketable" (i.e. an easy sell).

Unless you adamantly agree (and I mean you don't have an ounce of hesitation), then fine. But if you want your character to have a wife, a mistress, and a girlfriend, then go for it.

If your main character likes to shave her head and secretly loves a monk who owns a pet lizard, go for it. Everybody is not going to like it, but your audience will. Remember, you're not writing for Everybody.

Understand why.

Why do you want to tell stories? Why do you want

to write? Only you know the answer. If it's just for fame and fortune, then what I'm saying won't mean anything to you. But if you want to add your unique voice to a fascinating conversation or start one of your own, then do so.

Why do I write? Aside from the fact that I can't help myself, I want Somebody to know that they're not alone. I want my stories to show that we're all connected even if we live different lives, sometimes vastly different lives, and I'm here to say that's okay. Unique is beautiful. I know that Everybody doesn't agree, but I'm not writing for him.

In a wonderful blog post "Writer vs. The World," author Tracy Hickman states, "It's a big world out there—but you don't need the whole world to succeed as a writer."

Remember, your job as a writer isn't to write about or for Everybody or worry about Nobody. You're to write about Somebody. Because Somebody matters. Everybody may not like what you've written, but Somebody will.

Just to give you a real-life example, I recently published a book some people told me Nobody would read. Well, Somebody is buying the book and paying me quite well...

Update 2021: The monoculture, the mass media, is dead. Its time has passed. Trying to mimic the level of success of creators from the twentieth century is silly. (Plus when you study how much power the gatekeepers had based on a system of scarcity, you realize you're in a totally different world. Thank goodness.) We're sort of getting away from the mass market mentality but still tend to act as if it matters. Books, shows, music don't hit the same heights as those in the past when the markets were more controlled.

However, some writers still turn to a traditional publisher thinking they somehow have a magic bullet that allows them to reach a wider audience than an indie publisher ever could, completely ignoring that many indies have their books in libraries while traditional authors don't, and that there's presently a major distribution disruption that indies are nimble enough to get around that traditional publishers are struggling with. Their reputation makes many writers blind to their weakness. Unfortunately, I think it will take awhile for that myth to die.

All I can suggest is to continue to watch the major changes in other industries like music, movies/TV, and others. They're usually ahead of publishing and show where we're heading. Napster, the rise of digital music, and the collapse of Tower Records is a good case study.

CULTIVATE YOUR OWN GARDEN
Posted 2012

I've been told I'll never be a top blogger because I'm not angry enough. I don't call writers idiots or stupid. I don't say agents are a**holes or editors are morons. Nope, and I'm not going to. I'm too happy. I don't have time to deal with other people's venom.

I don't care about being popular. If a couple of people can get ideas and a few chuckles from what I've written, that's fine with me. I don't have time for comments (mostly spam anyway), and those who really want to talk to me know how to reach me. So what does that have to do with "Writers are Crazy"?

Crazy Lesson #7

Artists create and use their creation as communication.

Writers communicate and think it's creation.

. . .

A lot of writers get involved in online catfights and don't get to work. A number of people want me to talk about the Department of Justice lawsuit, others want me to comment on a top author who said that romance authors deserved to be paid peanuts, some want me to be either for or against traditional publishing, some want me to comment on how Amazon is going to rule the world and destroy publishing—AHHH!

Sorry, but I'm too busy for debates or trying to change opinions. If you don't like what I have to say, I know you're not reading this, because there's no place for you to vent. Like my books, my goal is to attract people like me. We're basically content with life, find humor in our quirks, and do our best.

Sure, I've read opinionated posts by other authors, and I am fascinated (impressed) by how much energy they spend to interact with some of the vile sent their way. And all of these authors—whether I agree with what they say or not—understand the artist's secret: create something.

A blog post, an article, instructions to follow, insight. No, they won't get paid for it, and it may not help sell their work, but they realize they are still creating.

Unfortunately, most writers don't understand the distinction. And those are the writers who comment on the blogs, send emails to other authors blasting someone or asking an opinion, complaining on loops or posting on forums. Sure, they're writing, but they're not creating anything. Yes, they're communicating, but it's the same as a person going into a museum and looking at a Mondrian and saying, "The coloring is all wrong. He should have done it this way..." So what?

If you really feel that way, then you do it!

In the early seventies when my mother wanted to share her dismay about starvation in the Horn of Africa, she created this beautiful painting depicting what was happening. It horrified some, intrigued others, but she got her point across. She used her art to make a point.

In his satirical novel *Candide*, Voltaire's hero travels the world and has extraordinary adventures only to return home and see the peace and contentment of a farmer. Candide decides, *"Let us cultivate our garden."*

I know there are many interpretations of this statement, but my interpretation is this: instead of ruminating on theories, focus on what you can *do*.

HOW TO REGAIN YOUR SANITY

"Work without disputing...it is the only way to render life supportable."

— VOLTAIRE, CANDIDE

Use your art (your writing) to make a point that lasts.

Fighting, blasting, pettiness has its place, but they are not lasting. Sure, we can read the letters of top authors and laugh at some of their pettiness, but what has lasted is their work—when they used their fueled passion to entrance us.

Whether you liked the controversial author Christopher Hitchens or not, he got his point across because he wrote his opinions as a coherent whole through articles and books. Some writers forget that. Reacting to what someone else says by sending a ranting comment isn't making art. Tweeting isn't making art. Going into the depths of your thoughts and putting them out there through showing, shipping, producing, or publishing your work—that's making art and a difference.

Bestselling author, Seth Godin, makes a great point about this in his post titled "What Are You Leaving Behind?"

Do what matters to you.

Stop complaining, arguing, fighting, and whining (unless it fuels your art somehow). A debate never changed the world. It's all about a lot of small actions. That's where your power lies. Don't just speak your convictions, live them. If you hate Amazon, then don't buy from them; don't publish with them. Stay away from them. It's that simple. If you hate self-publishing, stop. If you love it, don't stop. If you adore traditional publishing, keep doing it. If it's withering your soul, quit. If you like both indie publishing and traditional, go and have a ball. Do what works. You don't need a consensus in order to act. Multi-published, award-winning author Kristine Kathryn Rusch addresses this issue in the post "You Asked for My Opinion",where she discusses how to look at working with various business like PayPal, Amazon, and the like.

Understand the difference between creation and communication.

A number of writers confuse typing an email with writing a short story or essay, but it's not the same. It's easy to whittle time away on transient things: answering email, commenting on blogs, commenting on social media posts, tweeting, and the like. But the fact is you're just part of the noise of someone else's creation. You're shining a light on someone else's work instead of your own. It's okay to do, but understand that the individual who creates the blog has created a bigger impact than the person who reacts to it. Now, if you create a thoughtful blog in response...that's a different story.

So cultivate your garden. Tend to it. It's what makes your soul bloom and makes life truly interesting.

Update 2021: More than ever we need people culti-

vating gardens rather than torching the earth. Unfortunately, nowadays people are confusing attention with interest. Just because someone is briefly paying attention to something doesn't mean they care enough to act. The media is teaching some people that being loud, bombastic, and everywhere is the best way to market your brand. Some creators (musicians, performers, writers) following this model may find their names in different media outlets, but that doesn't mean they are selling tickets, seeing their books sold, etc. There is still power in reaching a loyal audience and delighting them. Better yet, they will do the selling for you.

THE WHINE OF WHY

2021

More often than not, writers come off as wimps. Not because they are, but because of how we behave. We crumble in the face of rejection, wither at the acidic words of critics, cower at the feet of agents and editors, and bemoan our wretched fate with a drink in our hand and a cigarette between our lips. Okay, some of this depiction is based on media portrayals, but sadly I've also seen it up close. Writers like to whine.

Crazy Lesson # 8

Artists find reasons to do something.
Writers find reasons not to do something.

Writers have a terrible habit of coming up with excuses —I mean reasons—why they shouldn't (or couldn't) do something.

"I can't write mysteries because I'm a literary writer."

"I can't ask for money because I'm bad with numbers." (I'm not making this up.)

"I can't indie publish because then no one will take me seriously."

"What if I write something new that nobody likes? I couldn't bear that."

As a creator it is your job to create. That means the past has little to do with the future.

Imagine a painter saying, "I can't do oils because I usually do watercolors."

"I can't use charcoal because all my work is in colored pencils."

"I failed algebra so I won't ask for more than a hundred dollars for my latest work."

Writers (I think because they deal with words) label themselves and then lock themselves into the labels.

Just because you did a particular behavior in the past does not mean you are wedded to it for eternity.

HOW TO REGAIN YOUR SANITY

Labels belong on cans, not people.

Judge yourself by what you do, instead of what you did. If you wrote literary fiction but now write fantasy, you are writing fantasy. You don't have to call yourself a "fantasy author." I am going to go out on ledge and say you don't call yourself anything. All the genre labels are for marketing; they don't belong in your creative realm. A friend of mine can jump from painting in acrylics to drawing wacky cartoons and then back to doing sophisticated pencil sketches. They don't stop and ask, "What kind of artist am I?" They create, then put it on the market under the different media. You can do the same. You're a writer first. A writer can write whatever they want to.

Thank your former self.

They gave you a lot. But you don't have to stay there. You can graduate. Imagine being forced to repeat the third grade over and over again. Well, that's what you're doing to yourself when you get stuck on one level. You've learned some skills. Now you can move on and do something else.

Try to create more than you consume.

You won't be able to, but it's a fun challenge, and it will get you out of your head. If you see a movie and you wanted to change the ending, write a novel, story, or poem in response. Think of the entertainment industry as one great conversation you can contribute to.

You have so many observations that the rest of us may have missed or never thought of. It is your job—a fun job—to see what's out there and turn it into something more or different or whatever. Let your imagination take flight. When you're busy working on your next project, you won't have time for the limit of labels. You will be free.

Face the fear.

I know this is a hard one. The reason many writers come up with excuses—I mean reasons—not to venture into new territories is the big F monster. It is real, and I in no way mean to belittle it. It's trying to keep you safe.

But the arts aren't meant to be safe. The arts, as a collective whole, are meant to make us feel something; to make another person feel an emotion—delight, terror, tension—involves risk. The risk of getting it wrong, unintentionally offending, being misunderstood.

That's part of the work. The audience you're meant to serve needs you to bring your best but also your humanity. Let us see who we are with all our beauty and flaws. Many of us are hurting, scared we need escape. Entertain us.

Think like an athlete.

I have a chronic condition that can knock me out for weeks if I'm not careful.

If you also have a chronic health condition that can

be debilitating, I have a special message for you: stop talking about it.

I understand it's frustrating. I know how painful it can be to see all the opportunities available and be physically unable to do them. To see all those amazing marathon runners when all you can manage is a sprint to the end of the block, if that. But please, instead of being envious, focus on what you can do.

You'll surprise yourself. You're not here to impress anyone. Just create the work. Think about the audience that will benefit from your work. Do your best. Then do it again and again. It adds up. If you can only manage five minutes, do it. Don't waste time wishing, dreaming, envying. It doesn't do you or your work any good.

I've written books in the pockets between agonizing pain. My readers will never know. I never want them to know. I know how fortunate I am that I get to entertain people who will pay me to do so. There's enough pain out there; if I can spread a little joy, that's plenty.

So when you're feeling down, be careful not to compare yourself to healthy writers. Get inspired instead. When I see a writer do something I find impressive that I physically can't do, I adjust it for my capabilities. It's a fun challenge and helps me get things done. I also ask for help when I need it.

The more you talk about your limitations, the more they're yours, the bigger they'll grow and will blind you to all the amazing things you can do now.

I know it's not easy, but it's not supposed to be. But

forging ahead in a healthy manner you can manage, no matter how small, will separate you from the others, those who spend whatever energy they have telling the world who they could have been if given the chance.

Remember you're always right.

This isn't about being right or wrong.

Replace "I can't" with "I won't," then ask yourself, "Why not?" Own your fears and your choices because they are yours. This isn't about blame, but responsibility. Consider an imaginary conversation like this:

You:"I won't ask for more money because I'm bad with numbers."

Your other self: "Why?"

You: "Because I don't want to look silly."

Your other self: "How much does this career matter to you?"

Then go on from there.

Be more afraid of stopping than failing.

You'll make mistakes. That's okay. But stopping, letting your fears, excuses, life, get in the way of writing? That will be painful. Taking a break to reassess is fine. Pausing due to health, financial issues, family issues, perfectly logical. Stopping completely? Dangerous. We'll all run out of time eventually. Some sooner than others. No excuse can protect you from that reality. Don't take time for granted.

Find your reason to try and then go do it.

WHERE YOU STAND
2021

Crazy Lesson # 9
Artists believe in standing out.
Writers believe in fitting in.

> **"Standing out takes time, money and confidence."**
>
> — SETH GODIN

I remember when I took a course in communication and came across a marvelous marketing tool called "individual conformity." Basically it's making people believe they're doing something that others aren't. It's how tribes are formed. So the hip stay-at-home parent makes sure their kids are dressed in X or are named Z, and before you know it, you go to a school and half the students are named Z and wearing X clothes.

It's why in school certain groups look the same, why you'll rarely see a rocker sporting bright pink.

Being part of the crowd is good for identification, but it can also be a straitjacket. Just because you like sports doesn't mean you can't play the flute.

Writers tend to fall in line here, too. When indie publishing became more accepted, instead of questioning why publishing looked the way it did, they just mimicked the bigger publishers but on a smaller scale.

The amount of writers who will shoehorn a perfectly good standalone novel into a series—because series sell—makes me sad.

It may take longer, but there are plenty of readers who like standalone novels. They like short stories. They like different characters.

Many readers won't even know what they like until you show it to them. But if you keep giving them what they've always gotten, is there any surprise when they grow bored?

Now, please don't misunderstand. This has nothing to do with expectations. I think it's very sloppy and disingenuous when a creator tries to "change" a genre. Adding a tragic ending to a romance because "that's real life" or leaving the work without an "ending" because the only true ending is death is just unfair.

You're in a contract. Just as if you were writing a story for a five-year-old you won't add grotesque, sexually explicit content "because you felt like it." The constraints in the arts is what also makes it fascinating.

BUT

When you respect and understand the expectations, why things are done a certain way and then you question it and add to enhance the reader's experience, that's golden. Realize it may not always work. But that's the point. That's where the magic begins.

HOW TO REGAIN YOUR SANITY

Be careful of what's always been done.

Question why it's always been done. There can be many good reasons. Series do sell well. Certain tropes are very popular. Can you do a fun spin on it?

Understand conformity's power.

It can be very lonely on your own. Trust me, I know. There were certain things I've been asked to add to my work to make it sell more, but while I may get a larger audience, I'd have to abandon the loyal audience I have. It's a value choice. It's your choice. Remember that.

It can take time. So much in the publishing industry is about speed. How fast you can build your mailing list, make a living, hit a bestselling chart. But to be the individual you are, to show the world all that you have to offer, will take time. Not everyone—some blaze fast and stay. For others, it's a slow burn. You may be somewhere in the middle. But think beyond your first or sixth book. What are all your interests? What does the world not know yet? Start building towards that. Otherwise you may never get there.

Quit what isn't working.

I'll say it plain. A writer is someone who writes. A publisher is someone who publishes. How you write or publish is a choice. Someone who tells you "how" has no business in your life. Your process is none of anyone's business as long as it works.

Make sure it's sustainable. But because everyone is doing it doesn't make it right for you.

Know the difference between "everyone is doing it" and "best practices."

This distinction trips up a lot of people.

I'm going to try to break it down. "Everyone is doing it" belongs (with certain caveats) to groupthink.

"Best practices" (with certain caveats) belongs to the individual.

Something "everyone is doing" can be best practices. But it's not always vice versa.

An example:

I went to a party and a friend offered me a drink.

Fine. I had one. She laughed when I nursed that one drink all night. Everyone gets drunk at these parties.

Fine, then I'd be the exception. Getting drunk—as a female—can be filled with hidden (and not-so-hidden) dangers. I was going to be the one who stayed sober and made sure my friends made it home safely.

Best practice. Having a sober driver. Not everyone does it, but it works. You still have fun and increase the likelihood you'll make it home in one piece.

There is a certain tribe that kills babies depending on how their baby teeth grow in. There are those trying to eradicate this practice, but it still stubbornly persists. This I put under "everyone is doing it." The reasons are varied. There are plenty of practices people are afraid to stop for fear of being ostracized, having opportunities taken, and the like. I understand that, but I hope I've made it clear that this is more of a groupthink ideology instead of a "best practice."

Some parents don't teach younger kids to floss with the idea that the baby teeth will just fall out and the adult ones will grow in. I won't get into all the logistics, but think about what the child is learning. They won't develop the habit of taking care of their teeth, which can lead to trouble in the future.

I have seen lives altered, changed, even lost due to certain practices that "everyone does" (and yes I'm being purposefully vague). If you take a moment to think of your own community, I'm sure you can point to similar behaviors that may not be as drastic as the one mentioned above but are accepted without question that may or may not be harmful.

Everyone is doing it versus best practices is not an easy road. It challenges you to question a lot (are you beginning to see a pattern here?), but it will help you to see what path you're heading down. Whether it benefits you or someone else.

Belonging matters but not too much.

Writers can be very tribal. Stupid discussions like what tools to use, outline versus no outline (you really have the time to care?). "Those on high" will dictate what a "real writer" is or does. Ignore them. We're all different, but again, my basic premise is this: a writer is a person who writes. How they write is not my concern. You don't need to worry, either, especially when it gets in the way of creating.

HIRING STRANGERS

2021

I was going to call this chapter "Professionals Hiring Amateurs," but I thought that was a little harsh, so I changed my mind. However, one thing that surprises me is how very trusting writers are. No matter what profession they were in in their other life, the moment they enter the writing world, they are as open and trusting as babes.

Crazy Lesson #10

Artists hire professionals to handle business matters. Writers hire amateurs to handle business matters.

This stuns me the most. I have yet to meet an artist who I can blithely convince to hand over their portfolio and let me manage their careers, but writers do it all the time.

Okay, I have something to confess. I've had seven agents. Three of them I made up. I wanted to run an experiment. At the time, after twelve traditionally published books, I couldn't believe that no editor would give me the time of day unless I hired someone else to speak on my behalf, so I made up an agent and got my calls answered, emails replied to and so on. They were courteous and kind to this no-name agent, while completely dismissive of me as a writer. This was awhile back, but it left a lasting impression on me.

I didn't have to prove anything. Nothing! Like a con artist, I just acted the part and was given the authority. I fooled one publishing professional I was working with who thought I needed an agent and wouldn't work with me otherwise, so I made one up. They didn't even check for a business card or website. The fake agent had neither. But it didn't matter! I had an agent and now somehow I was "legit."

Please let that sink in.

I realized I could go to writing conferences and say I was an agent and no one would check. At a small conference, I tested this out. I'd been mistaken for an agent—heaven knows why—and decided to play with it. Some writers actually wanted me to represent them. They'd just take me at my word! I kept waiting for someone to at least whip out their phone and do a simple search for Ima Kidding. (Okay, no, that wasn't one of my made-up names, but I was tempted.)

Unfortunately, I have a sinking suspicion that even

without any credentials on top of no business cards, website, or history of clients, I could have BS'd my way to get them to trust me. Even when I told people I'm just a writer, they would still suggest I try being an agent. Based on what? I can send work to editors? I look at contracts?

I'm not here to do agent bashing—they have a host of other troubles to deal with in this new world, and they're just a symptom of a bigger broken system.

I want to touch on the idea of hiring strangers, because for some reason, above hiring a CPA or literary lawyer, two fields that have set industry requirements, hiring an agent is of utmost importance to many writers. There are savvy writers who have good working relationships with agents, but most writers have no idea what they're getting into. When hiring strangers, there are certain things to consider and understand, because many writers don't realize how many people profit—I mean benefit—from their insecurities.

HOW TO REGAIN YOUR SANITY

Verify.

Referrals are your friends. But still verify. Just because it's your best friend's nephew doesn't mean he should have access to your checking account. What are their credentials? Do they have any? Are they legitimate?

. . .

You are smarter than you think.

May I suggest that instead of doubting yourself, you doubt others more? It's a tiny shift in focus. Instead of inward, it's outward.

Genteel doubt (skepticism's more refined cousin) can be very useful to keep you from falling for some of the unethical and sometimes ignorant behaviors of "experts."

Sure running a business can be overwhelming, but if someone else can learn something, so can you. You will forget certain details, you will make mistakes, but you will also learn, so when you hire someone they can't pull the wool over your eyes. There are people eager to exploit your ignorance. Sure, they'll handle your money, sure, they'll handle your publishing rights—and, if you're not diligent, they'll help themselves to what you're not paying attention to.

Be careful of anyone who says, "Don't worry about it."

If you're worried, you have a reason. Don't understand your payment? Your contract? Anything? Ask.

If they can't give you a satisfactory answer, they may not know what they're doing or they're hiding something. Your concerns are valid. For some reason, writers have been taught otherwise. I had an editor get really annoyed with me when I asked about a certain direction the publishing imprint was going. I wasn't too surprised when the line was eventually closed.

Ask questions.

I know I've said this before, but it's important. You learn by asking questions. However, when working with someone or before you even start, consider asking "how" instead of "why." For example, "How did you come to this decision?" will give you a lot more insight into their decision making than, "Why do you think that?"

It's similar to math class when you had to show how you got to a solution rather than just showing the answer. I grew up with an engineer; trust me, this approach really forces you (and others) to defend your ideas based on evidence rather than emotion. When it comes to running your business, you want one more than the other.

Check your ego.

Flattery has gotten some writers in more trouble than I care to think. People who want to distract you from the truth will sometimes—many times—tell you what you want to hear. Don't fall for anyone telling you that you're the greatest, wittiest, most brilliant writer ever, that your work will be a bestseller translated into languages both in this universe and others. Keep your ego in check, and sharpen your BS meter.

Check your insecurities.

Anyone who puts you down, dismisses you, makes you feel stupid—walk away, cut ties. It's only the beginning of nasty things to come.

Remember whoever you hire works for you, not the other way around.

Imagine hiring a babysitter who dictates to you the terms of their service. You pay them and they do whatever they want to do. Most parents would give up date night until they found a babysitter willing to work within their requirements.

Keep that in mind for your own working relationships.

This is a business transaction meant to be mutually beneficial. You do not need to be grateful. Whoever you decide to work with is not doing you any favors. Be very careful about mixing friendship with professionalism. That's how many writers get taken.

Hire others for what they can do for you. You're the content creator, many businesses (i.e. agents, if you decide to use one, editors, publicists, etc.) wouldn't exist without you, so think of yourself at the top of the pyramid rather than at the bottom. That shift in thinking will help you see your working relationships in an entirely new way.

THE ORIGINATOR

Crazy Lesson #11

An artist knows originality is for suckers.
A writer thinks originality is everything.

An artist knows what came before.

They study the masters. Most people have seen an image of an art student in a museum looking at a painting and copying it. My mother reveled in those outings. Still does. She delights in finding and noticing new techniques. You don't have to come out fully formed; your personal style will emerge as it moves away from copying into something that is uniquely you.

Artists know other artists and their styles whether the works of Maud Lewis or Tom Feelings or Claude Monet.

For writers, there seems to be a lack of interest in the history or appreciation for the art of storytelling.

They think that because some top editor says that what comes across their desk is turgid and unoriginal that they must seek out to write something that has never been done before. That stress has stopped the imagination of many.

Originality comes when a creative person sees what's there and fearlessly, boldly, naively, imaginatively puts their own spin on it. That's it.

One way to accomplish this is to study who came before. I'm no longer surprised to meet a North American young person who doesn't know who Charles Dickens is. But I *am* surprised by a writer who tells me they've seen one of the more than 100+ movie renditions of *A Christmas Carol* and can't tell me what novella it was based on (the title being a clue), let alone who the author was. I've met writers who don't know that *Fences, The Joy Luck Club, Monster, Life of Pi,* or *Black Panther* started out as novels/plays/comics. (Granted, some of the ignorance is due to snobbery and total disinterest, but that's a completely different issue.)

No curiosity.

A lack of curiosity can be deadly to your storytelling.

Curiosity waters imagination, which leads to originality because originality comes from being unapologetically you.

HOW TO REGAIN YOUR SANITY

Copy the masters.

Literally. Open up a book and type (or handwrite) a page or two, word for word, from an author you admire.

I learned this tactic years ago after reading the book *Fiction Writer's Brainstormer* by James V. Smith, and it made perfect sense to me. Again, when I took art classes, I imitated, copied, etc., so copying someone's writing felt comfortable and a reasonable way to learn and develop my skill.

By doing this practice, you will gain muscle memory and learn cadence, pacing, cliffhangers, and so much more that I can't even list.

Give it a go. No harm in trying.

"There can be no doubt that in art, no small portion of our task lies in imitation, since, although invention came first and is all-important, it is expedient to imitate whatever has been invented with success, and it is a universal rule of life that we should wish to copy what we approve in others."

— HEAD TEACHER OF RHETORIC IN ANCIENT ROME, MARCUS FABIUS QUINTILIANUS

Read a lot.

This gets overlooked a lot, and I'm not sure why. Reading is one of the best ways to study and build a storytelling vocabulary. Not everything will be to your taste. Don't study a work if you don't have the ability to separate taste from craft, but there are hidden gems of insight if you know how to learn this way.

Find inspiration from the past.

In *The Creative Habit* by Twyla Tharp, she discusses finding the original source of something.

This can be so much fun. See who influenced whom. See what inspired something else. (A song can inspire a play; a painting can inspire a short story, etc.) It's a treasure trove of insight.

Remember, originality is all about "origin," and with enough input that you mix and meld and then produce, the origin will be you.

Have the mindset of a scientist versus a critic.

I know it sounds strange. I've been harping on thinking like an artist and now I want you to think like a scientist? Yes.

Too often when writers are told to approach a

work, they come with a critical eye. They feel that they have to analyze and tear down something in order to see its inner works.

That rarely works. Imagine learning how to build a computer by dismantling it. Go ahead, I'll wait.

Not to pound on professors, I had many I enjoyed, but one thing I hated in English class was when the teacher would tell us what an author was thinking during a scene.

Um....how do you know they'd purposely put in the dying sun as a metaphor for death? How do you know that the necklace represents both consumerism and woman's subjugation? We as readers come to stories with our own filters and world views. There are some things you'll see in a story that a writer didn't intend, didn't see, or tossed in.

Criticism rarely helps you to see magic. What I suggest is approaching writing like a scientist.

First, most scientists approach problems with a sense of wonder.

Go to stories with a sense of excitement. If the story doesn't wow you, move on, unless you're disciplined enough to read works that aren't to your tastes and yet can still see the merit. Many long-term professionals can do this; newer writers have a harder time, so I suggest start with joy.

Okay, so the wonder is in place, right? You just finished reading something amazing. Now be prepared to lose some of that amazement. Unfortunately, when you pull the curtain away, some of the magic will be lost and you'll see the moving pieces. So be *very* careful about deep analysis. There are other ways to learn that won't ruin stories for you.

Try something and then forget it.

The subconscious is always filling your toolbox. If you become too aware of it, it starts to slip away, and the critical voice will take hold: "You call that a scene? You don't know how to…"

It takes practice. Keep going. Rarely—make that never—do my stories turn out the way I thought they would. But if they surprise me, I hope they surprise the reader, too.

Put a spin on it.

Just like musicians remix their songs, take one of your own stories and remix it for fun. Do it from another point of view. Remember, everything you do doesn't have to work or be published. There are some quick, funky stories I do just for me. That's fine, no one says you have to publish everything you write. If you want to, go for it. If you don't, fine. As long as you keep putting work out. Again, your process is your process. Anything that gets in the way needs to be reconsidered and/or discarded.

THE ROCK AND THE RIVER

2021

There is a dangerous lull of certainty in indie publishing. (There's a long-delayed shakeup in traditional publishing, but they're still acting with some "old world" thinking.)

Recently my blood turned cold when a writer told me they were so happy now that they had a "stable income." Okay, granted, with the indie world it's marvelous to get paid monthly. I remember when I used to plan my life around two or three cheques a year and scramble when an editor forgot to put in a request for payment. Monthly is good. But to consider writing a stable profession is unsettling.

There's a difference between making a living and building a career. Making focuses on the now, building focuses on the future. Naturally, you don't have to choose, this is not an either/or proposition, but it is important to make the distinction when you're making decisions.

Crazy Lesson #12

Artists revel in the realm of uncertainty.
Writers revel in the realm of certainty.

I remember when computers didn't have monitors. (I know that just blew some minds...take a deep breath.)

Yes, times have changed, and yet...I'll hear from people older than me (who should know better) that they can't wait for things to return back to normal.

This new world is normal. It's different, absolutely, but we're not going back to the way things were. Instead, we're moving ahead to the way things will be because times change.

Time keeps changing.

Change happens slowly or fast, but it happens.

Think about what the music and movie industry looked like ten years ago. How about twenty? Thirty?

How about some of the technology you use now? How many even existed fifteen years ago?

The moment you think of anything pertaining to your business as "stable," slap yourself.

It's stable for now, but nothing is permanent. Few things are certain. Technology, inflation, pandemics, wars...they're not going anywhere. They'll change, go dormant, but they'll rise again and shake up our world.

Plan for that.

HOW TO REGAIN YOUR SANITY

Don't think like a salaried worker.

You're a freelancer, entrepreneur, or both. However, you are not exchanging time for money. (That's what a day/night job is for.)

Thinking like a salaried worker may limit the vision you have for your work and your business. There are reasons businesses do quarterly reports, so that they can monitor the health of the business at least four times a year and see if there are trends or changes that might affect them.

Know that life happens.

Family concerns, health woes, market changes, unexpected losses, etc.: there may be a time in your life that you may not be able to write because some life event knocks you down. It happens. You'll get back if you give yourself the space to regroup and renew. To think it will never happen is planning for failure.

Study business.

Look around you. How many businesses that you grew up with are still the same? Are still even around? Why or why not? There are businesses that are able to weather change and ones that don't. You'll learn a lot from both.

I recently had an indie author brag to me that they're better off than the "poor traditional authors" because they don't have to sign contacts.

Um...I had to take a deep breath before I gently told them that every time they clicked "Agree," they were entering a contract.

Signing, clicking, shaking hands, verbal—never mind how it's done, if you don't know when you're entering into a contract, you need to do your homework. Now.

Otherwise, you just might "speak" or "click" (and a host of other ways) all your intellectual rights away.

Accept uncertainty.

There are so many things I don't know, but I learned that uncertainty is my friend. The moment I put a full stop in the place of a comma or a question, I've sabotaged my growth.

Uncertainty can keep you observant, opens your eyes; it allows you to let the wonder in.

Don't be too quick to accept what everyone does. What everyone thinks. Never think you know everything because you don't, and that's okay.

It's okay to be afraid, to feel all the emotions. That's what can fuel your work. Disappear into it, let us disappear into it.

It's in the shades of gray, the gaps where art emerges.

Let yours rise up and entertain us.
Happy writing.

INTRO TO BONUS CHAPTER

The following bonus chapter came into being due to the generous support of the Kickstarter backers who helped raise money for *Artists are Weird BUT Writers are Crazy*.

To you all, I send a heartfelt thank-you.

Enjoy!

THE CANVAS AND THE KEYBOARD

2021

Crazy Lesson #13
Artists see creating as a way of life.
Writers see creating as a way of making a living.

The canvas. The blank page. They are not sacred. They are not special. They are both neutral. One line or sentence, one brush stroke or line of color does not destroy anything. Both come as blank slates - what is created comes from the artist/writer. Nothing happens without their input, their thoughts, their ideas, their imagination. They are something to work with, not conquer (unless that kind of battle mindset works for you). Fear may whisper, but don't let it shout. Just begin without judgment.

"...being an artist means you'll always be

a little insecure and a little unsure, because you don't know where you're going a lot of the time—every act of creation is new. You may have feedback and there are moments when people will give you reassurance, but you won't have that always. But that's true of life in general, and people make too big a fuss over the struggles of being an artist, as though an artist's humanity is different from anyone else's, as though we are a different kind of creature. It's not. We are not. Keep going."

— WRITER/ARTIST ETEL ADNAN

How you approach your work is either with a gentle nudge or a hatchet. You get to choose. Will you be a flash in the pan or have a long-term career? It takes a strategy to survive the ups and downs of a long career. Luck is great, but savvy is better. You can create a writing career without burnout or depression, but there will be sacrifices.

HOW TO REGAIN YOUR SANITY

Manage your priorities rather than your time.

There are a lot of books about productivity and

time management, but for an artist, it can come down to one simple focus: your health, your family, your work. Everything else falls around that. Your work is part of your life, not something you "get to" after you've watched TV, massaged your social media accounts, and hung out with friends. It is a daily or weekly practice that is as routine as brushing your teeth. It is important. Not important as in "I'm a genius and nothing else matters" but important as "I need to get this done because it's important to me." You put in the time; you don't find it.

Understand that knowledge must be used.

When you're writing, keep out the critic, the bean counter, and the marketer. They have no place in this creative space. Your writing space needs to be a place of fun and freedom.

But it also needs to be a place of practice.

You can learn a lot of things, but if you never apply them, you might as well stay ignorant. Whenever my mother discovered a new technique, she immediately tried to replicate it, test it, study it until it became a part of her. Application is essential. That's why it saddens me when a writer keeps working on one piece over and over again. You can't grow and apply new knowledge on the same old piece. It's like a chef learning a new recipe but using the ingredients from an old one. Learn something new, use it, try it, keep it or discard it, and repeat. Project after project.

. . .

Remember that life happens.

Sometimes major life events take precedent over your writing. If writing is your main livelihood, put in barriers to plan for such events. For example, Agatha Christie tried to make sure to have an extra novel on hand so that she didn't have the financial pressure of creating during hard times.

So stock away a project if you can so that you have a buffer for life's waves. If you have to stop, stop. Your health, your family matter more. You can always get back to writing. If you can only write and not publish, that's fine as well. Publish later.

Careful how you view money and fame.

In the past, there was a strange sense of pride for writers who created books that didn't reach the masses. There was a coolness to being an underground hit, developing a cult following. But now, with many indies, money drives their work.

I get it. You have to decide the kind of business you wish to run. If you want to be a brand author, you will stay in one lane for your entire career and readers will know what to expect from you.

If you decide you want to write in other genres and experiment, you will have a longer journey to reach a certain level of success because you will be developing different audiences.

That's a business choice.

But writing? Writing and business are two different ways of thinking.

Even if it means going against your present brand and you want to write something else, do it. You can put it under another name if you want to (not that you need to in this new world, but again, that's a choice). Or stack them up and in several years publish them all at once and give a new readership a host of things to read.

My point is, when I see authors burning out because they think they have to work like a fiction factory, it's tragic and unnecessary. You can be prolific for decades if you follow your creative muse, not the beastly, competitive, driven money taskmaster.

And if you're not prolific? Who cares? Just keep putting out. Even one book a year for forty years gets you somewhere. I know there are people who can create forty books in one year. Again, so what? Stop worrying and do your own thing.

You need to understand how the system works and then work in a system that best serves you, your family, and your needs, not the other way around. It's the one key to a healthy, long-term career.

Value isn't what you think it is.

Because we are using short-term metrics, many writers are deeming their work useless because of present conditions. That's sad. Was the movie *The Shawshank Redemption* a bad movie in the theaters but suddenly great on VHS? How about Shakespeare's play about Romeo and Juliet? Was it no good when it was basically invisible for nearly seventy years while Thomas Otway's similar play with star-crossed lovers Lavinia and Romeo, in *The History and Fall of Caius Marius*, was vastly popular? You don't know when your work will hit the right audience. That may take time.

But don't deem it a failure by months or even years because you don't know what the future holds. Don't judge your work; it's not your job to. Your job is to create and let go.

Relationships can be tricky.

You may lose people. That's part of the creative journey. You'll outgrow some relationships, others will change, but that's normal.

Be careful who you expect to support you. Some people you care about will purposely withhold support; some truly don't understand your chosen profession. I grew up during the AIDS crisis, and the one thing that stood out for me as a kid was how many families abandoned their sick relatives.

So many people had to create "families of the heart" rather than "families of the blood." So people may think "blood is thicker than water," but if the blood is diseased, does it matter? Creating new families allowed people to die with dignity surrounded by love.

You may have to do the same. Find like-minded, like-hearted people. There's no shame in it. It's another brave act of freedom. Find the people who accept you. Sometimes the family you choose is healthier than the family you're born into. As a creator, that is something to keep in mind.

Trust the process.

You're smarter and more imaginative than you think. The problem is "thinking." Thinking can get in the way of so many fascinating, wondrous, and strange ideas. So face a new project and dive in. Don't think. Let the story tell itself. Let it surprise you. Let the words flow. Don't think, just feel. We are feeling beings first; that's what we're searching for. Emotions.

Trust the process. You'll find an answer. You'll come up with a solution. You may need to switch projects, take a walk, or take a nap, but it will come to you.

The reason for it all.

What's the point?

You have to answer that. The answer will guide your career. The writer who says, "I know this won't sell," and stops writing made it only about commerce.

The writer who enjoys the book they've written

and puts it on the market for others to find has a different narrative.

It takes a very strong personality to put money into the mix. If you start only using money as a measure, you're headed down a slippery slope if you don't make it clear that's what you're doing. That's all that matters. If you get bored writing the same type of book and yearn for something different, you'll have to be strategic or just accept that this is the life you've built and will stay with.

Writers have become too outcome focused. Too wedded to what happens with the work. For example, I recently heard an inspiring story by a successful writer who shared that at the university their professor told them there were lots of changes they needed to make to their work. The writer didn't like the idea and sent the manuscript out, as is, anyway and the work eventually sold for a lot of money. The moral of the story the writer wished to share was that trusting your gut and standing up for your work can lead to career and financial success.

I believe in that. But...I have a caveat. I would have applauded that writer even if they hadn't sold the book right away to a publisher that didn't give them a lot of money.

What if that same work landed on the wrong desk? What if the writer belonged to a group that is routinely dismissed or ignored?

Protect your work anyway. You may be wrong. So what? You learn and do better. I have my own story of people wanting to change aspects of my work. Yes, some suggestions would have made my work more "commercially viable," but I didn't want to do that. I think of Kevin Kwan of *Crazy Rich Asians* fame having to fight not to have a white woman cast in the lead role in the film version of his book. To me, even if the film hadn't been a big hit with an Asian cast, having an Asian heroine was already a win. Do you see where I'm going here?

Money isn't the only measure. Impact matters. Choice matters. Different voices and visions matter. A variation on a well-known theme matters.

As writers, we don't have to just follow the culture. We can influence it in tiny ways. If we want a future different than our past, we need to shake things up a bit, and that takes time.

Give yourself some time. The expectation of being wealthy in three years is hurting some people. Making a living is different than building a career.

I'm not talking about being a starving artist. Cash-flow matters. Business acumen matters. You should know how well certain projects are doing so you can spruce them up if needed or move on. Not everything will do well right now...or ever...but that's a long-term issue. I hope you'll be too busy with fascinating projects to care.

Give yourself permission to stretch your wings and not hear applause. Applaud yourself.

Learn how to stand alone. Even if it's a little bit, dip your toe in another opportunity others are ignoring.

You can be the little whisper we need, one that says, *Hey, did you see that?*

Not everyone will pay attention. You don't need everyone, just a few people, and slowly you'll have an audience waiting eagerly to hear what you have to say. Don't let them down. Stay consistent.

That's what artists do. They show up. They don't care about being the best; they care about making a difference, making art, or both. They entertain us. They surprise us. They help us see. They make us feel. Then they do it all over again.

Because the world needs it.

Because it makes life rich.

Because it's fun.

EXTRA

One of the best advice I ever got.

When I was in middle school, about twelve years old, for gym class that semester we had two choices: aerobics or wrestling. I decided to choose wrestling. (Don't ask me why.) At the time, girls couldn't wrestle with boys (don't know if that's still the case), therefore I was matched with the *only* other girl who decided to take wrestling, too. She was a junior lifeguard at our local pool who was beautifully built. She had broad shoulders, thick legs, and muscular arms.

I was built like a wet noodle.

There was no contest. She could pin me to the mat each and every time. She could lift me in the air and slam me to the ground like the Hulk did to Loki in *The Avengers*. All the guys would watch and wince. Sometimes they'd shout in sympathy.

She's lock me in a position until I was pounding the floor for mercy, and they'd go, *Ooooh!*

She'd drop me to the ground, and they'd say, *Awww!*

She'd swing me in the air and then drop me to the ground, and they went, *Damnnnnnn!*

That's what I heard for weeks as I got my face slammed to the mat and my arm twisted behind my back.

I lost over and over again. Swiftly and badly.

Until one day my coach/teacher took me to the side and told me something that changed my life. He said this: "You will *never* beat her, but you can outlast her. Make sure she never catches you."

It was as if a lightbulb went off in my head. He was right. Instead of being ashamed of being thin and wiry, I could use my "weaknesses" to my advantage. I could be like a snake and slip out of her grasp. And that's exactly what I did. I never let her get a good hold of me. I slipped out of her grasp; I moved quickly, easily, in unexpected ways. I stunned and frustrated her.

I never won, but I never lost, either.

I got to keep playing. I got to stay in the ring until my time was up, and I had a great time doing it.

That's how I approach my writing career. I don't care about winning or losing. I care about staying in the game and having a blast. I wish the same for you.

Use your own "weaknesses" to your advantage.
Hone your strengths.
Go and write with the heart and mind of an artist.
Have the time of your life.
In all our shared craziness, I'm rooting for you.
In your own special way, tell us a story.
Again and again.

ALSO AVAILABLE

The Writer Behind The Word: Steps to Success in the Writing Life.

10 Things to Forget: to be Creatively Free

ABOUT THE AUTHOR

Dara Girard is an award-winning, national bestselling author of more than fifty books.

She has written numerous articles for *Byline* magazine, *The Writer's Notebook*, *Romance Writers Report*, newsletters and e-zines. She has also interviewed many industry professionals on the Novelists Inc blog.

Visit her website at www.daragirard.com.

You can write her at:
contactdara@daragirard.com

or

Dara Girard
PO Box 10345
Silver Spring, MD 20914

If you would like to receive a reply, please send a self-addressed, stamped envelope.

www.ingramcontent.com/pod-product-compliance
Lightning Source LLC
Chambersburg PA
CBHW062034120526
44592CB00036B/2092